d

nds & Letters 6

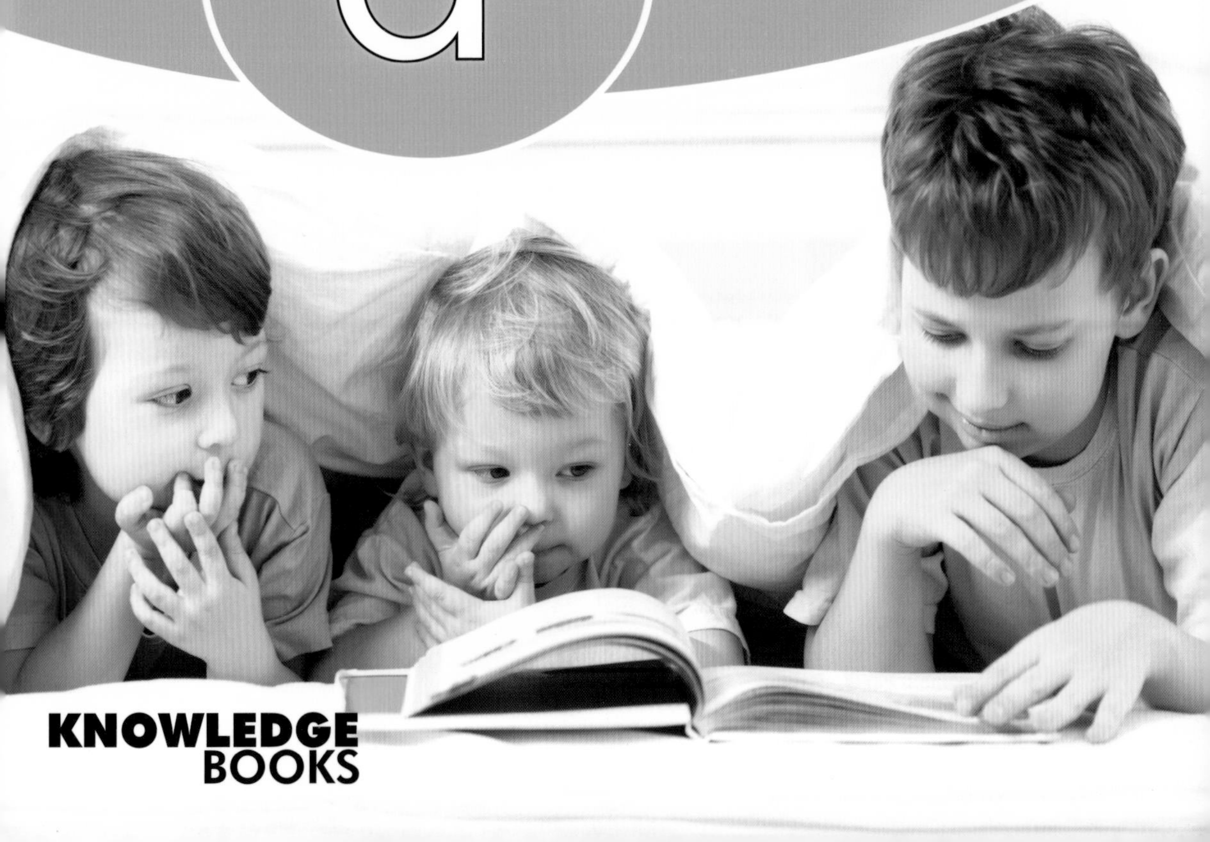

KNOWLEDGE
BOOKS

doll	duck
dress	dad
dig	dish
dog	

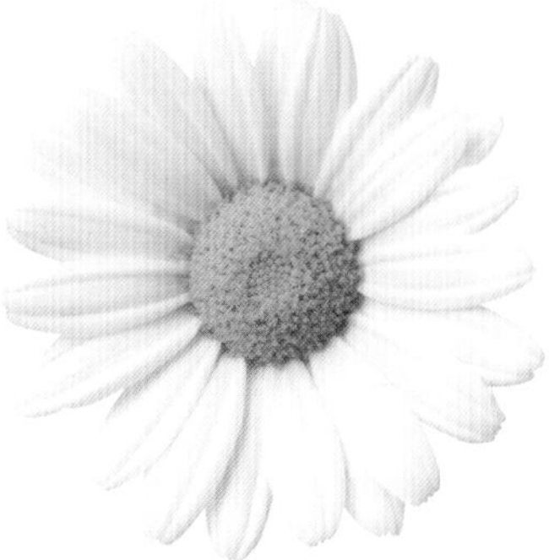

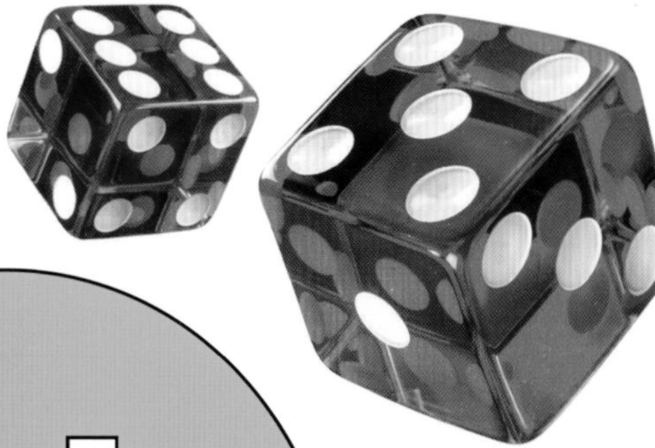

d

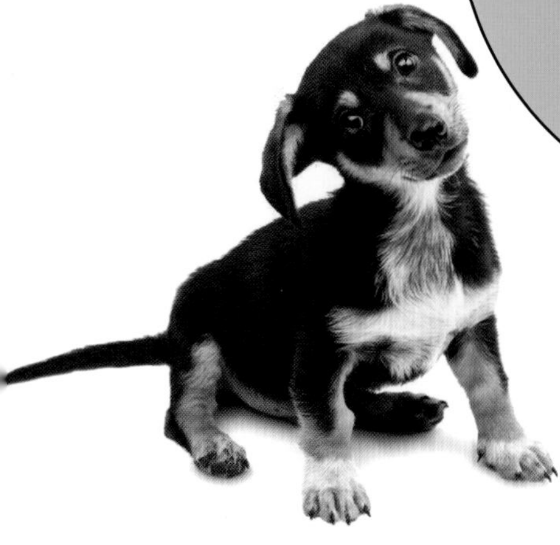

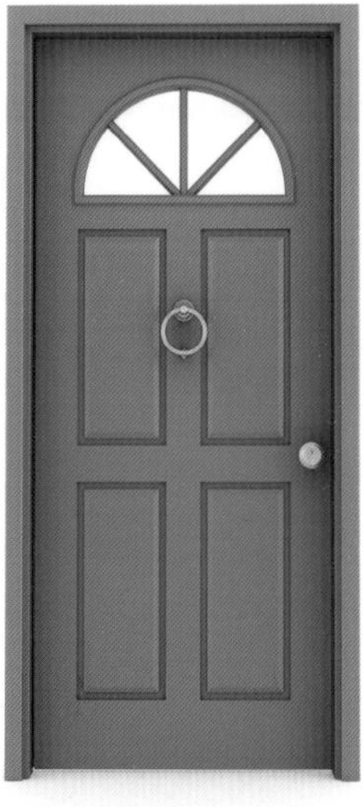

doll

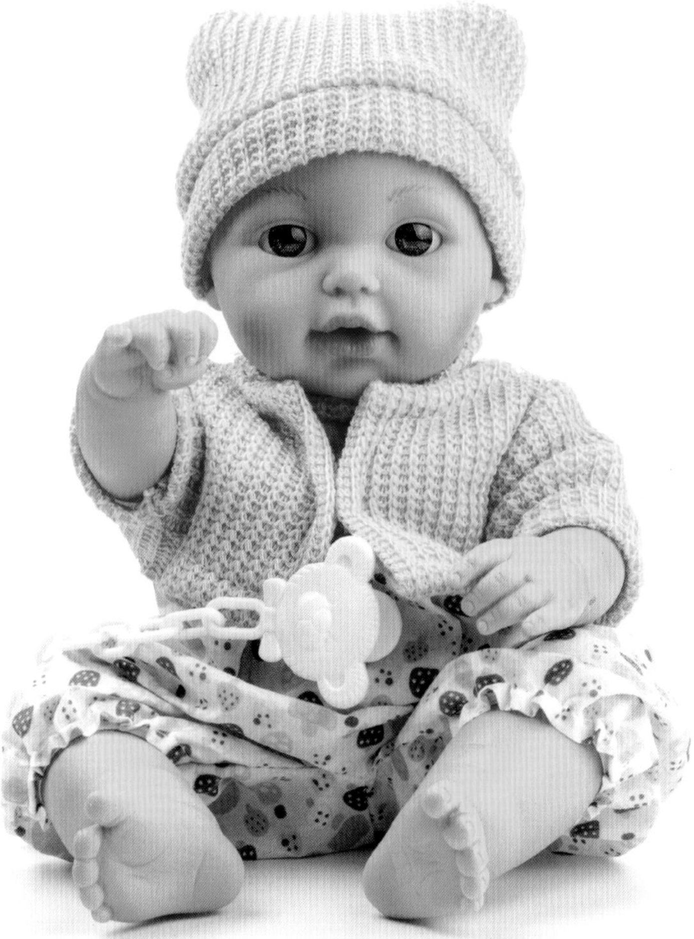

duck

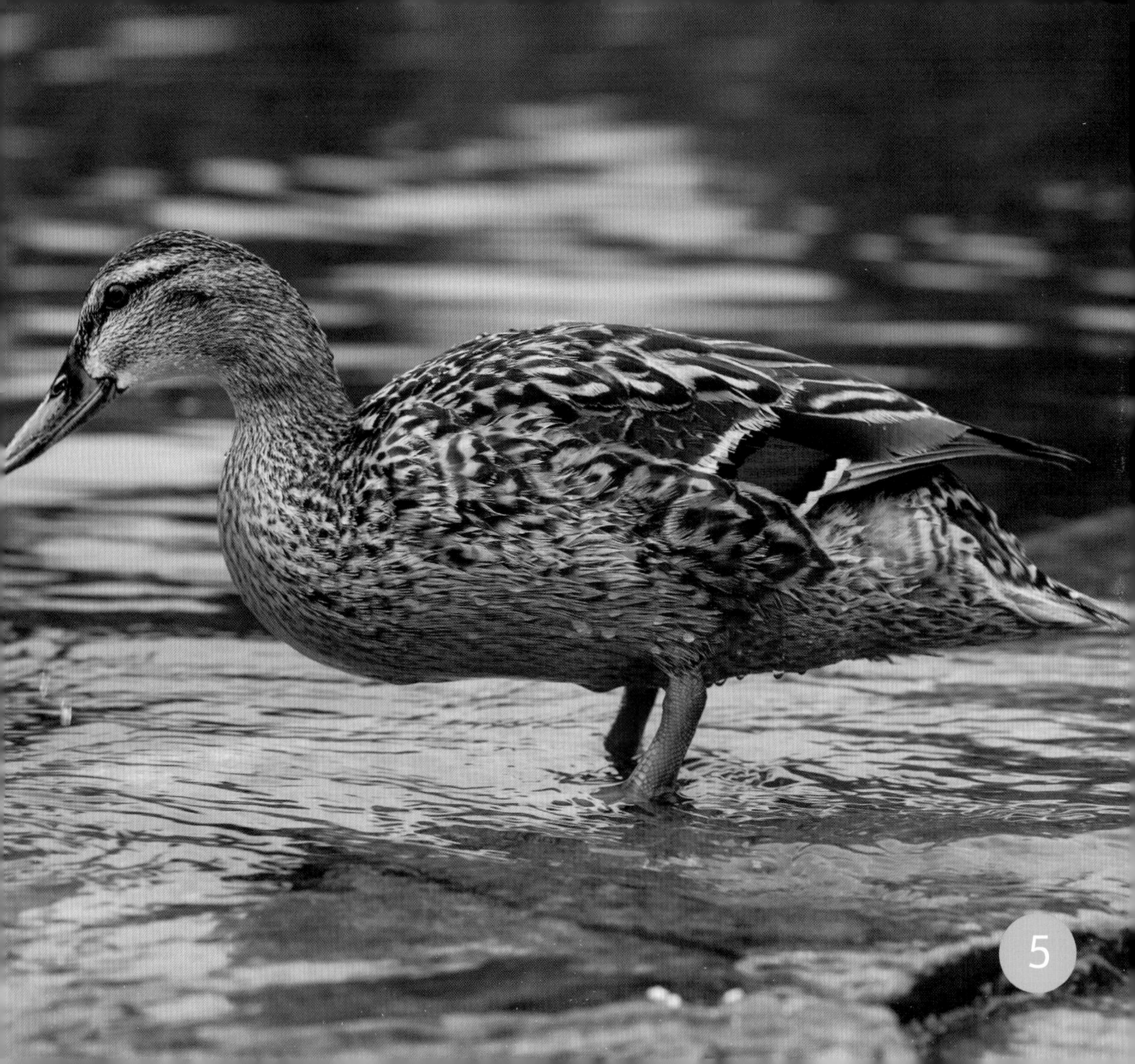

dress

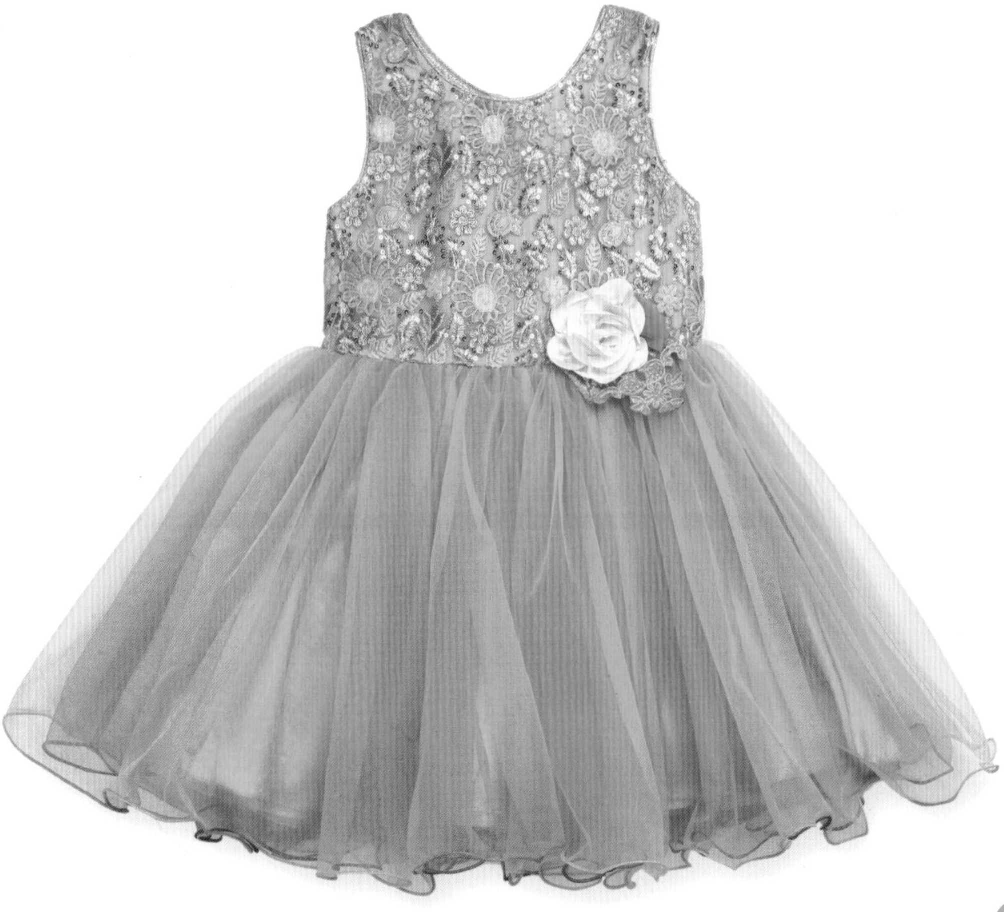

dad

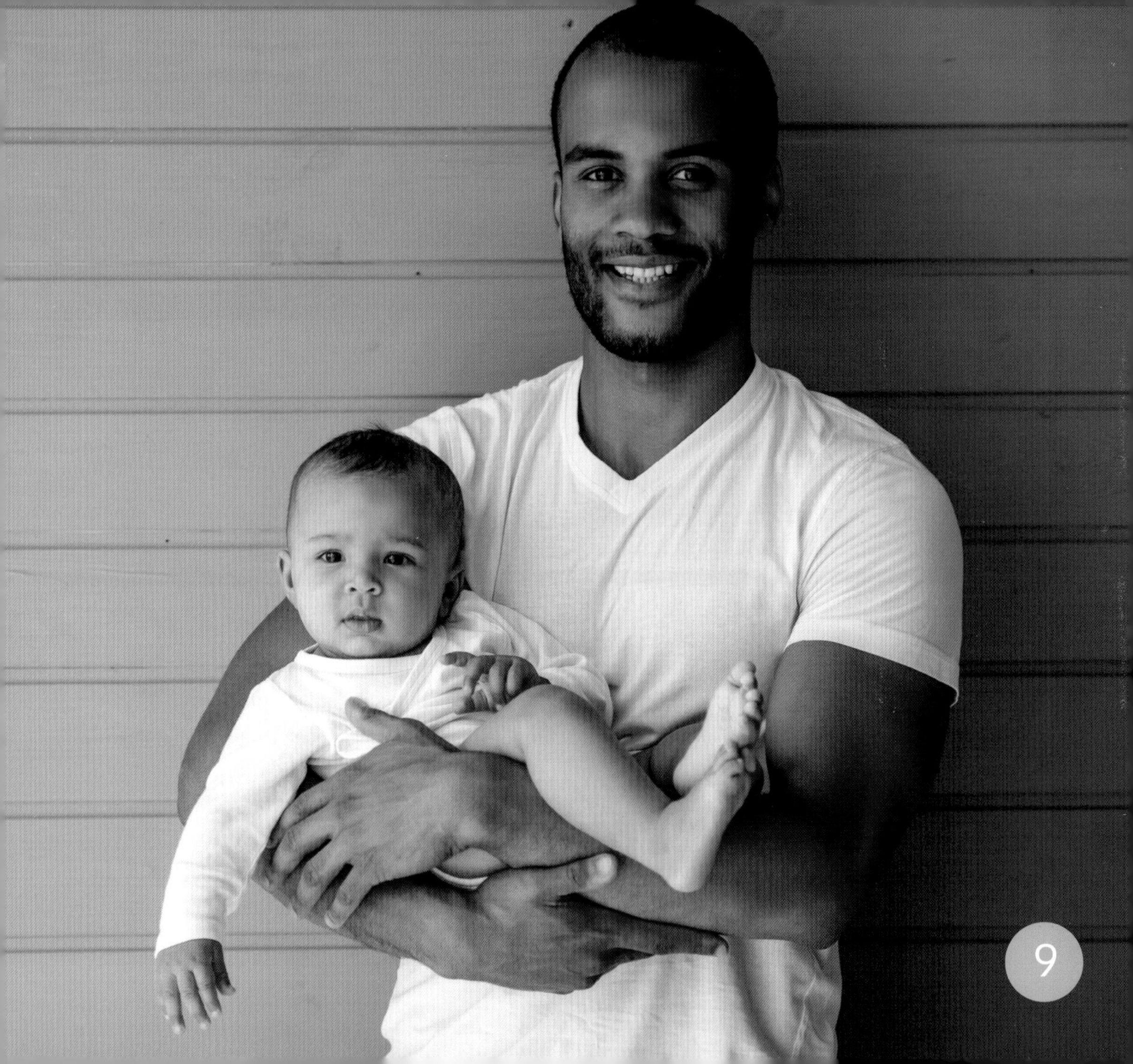

dig

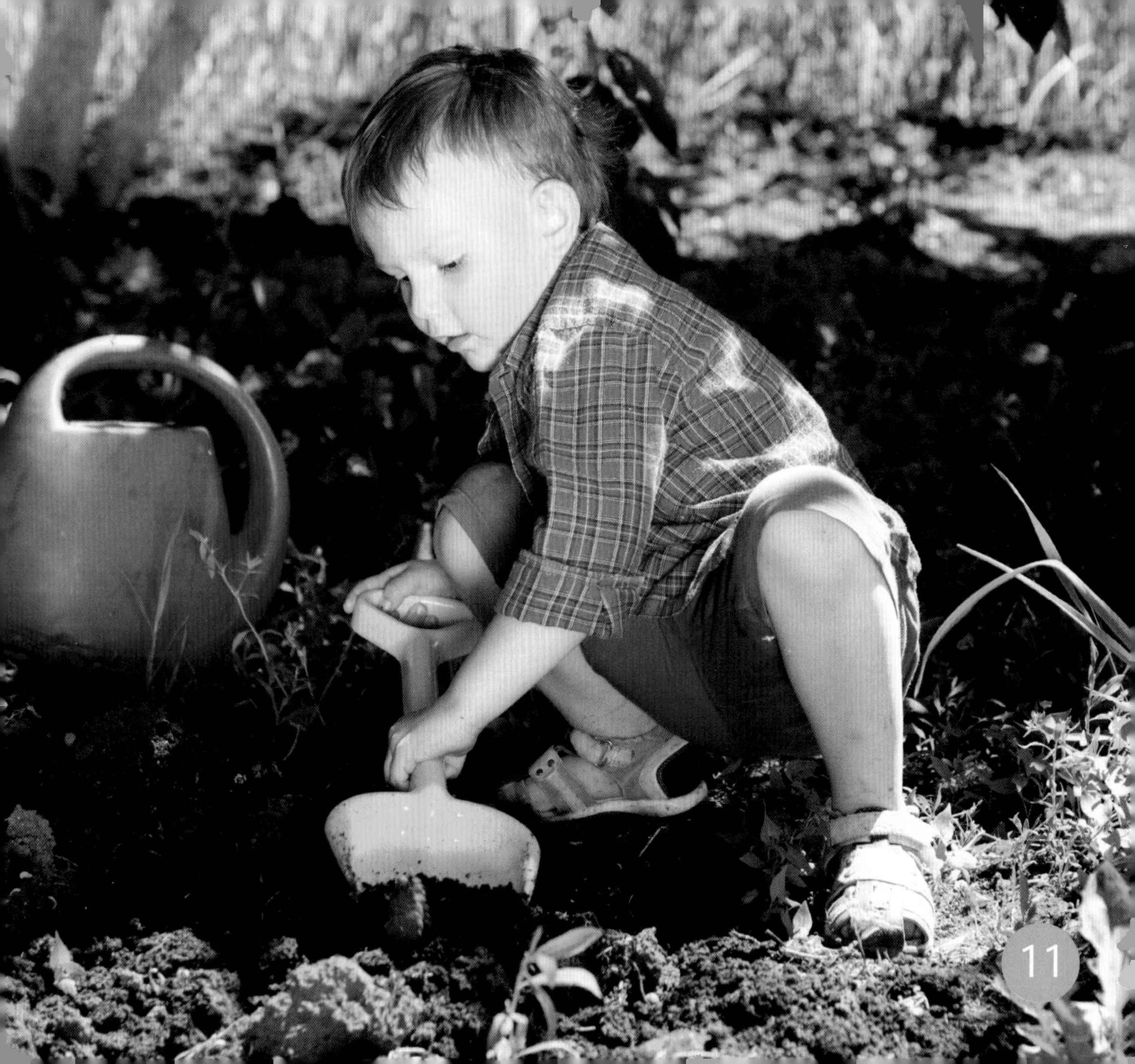

dish

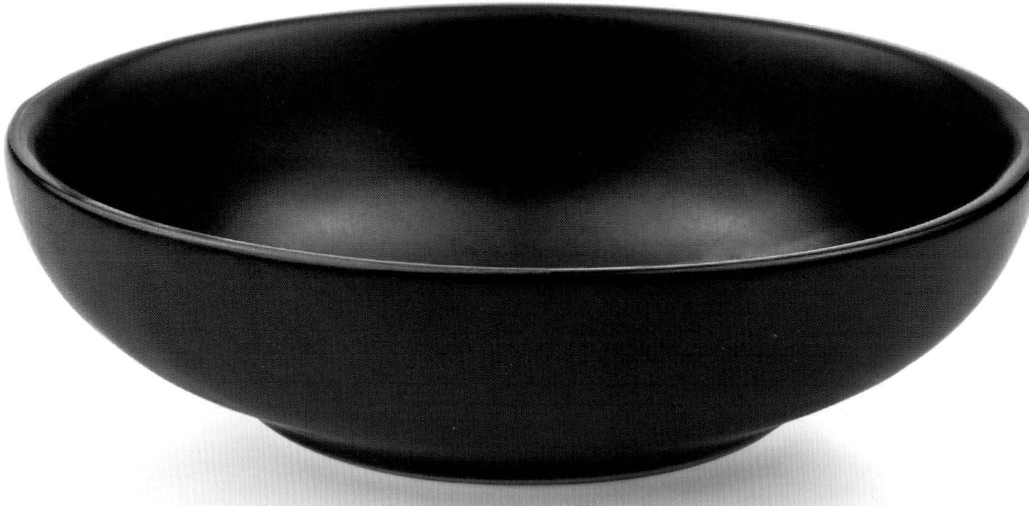

dog

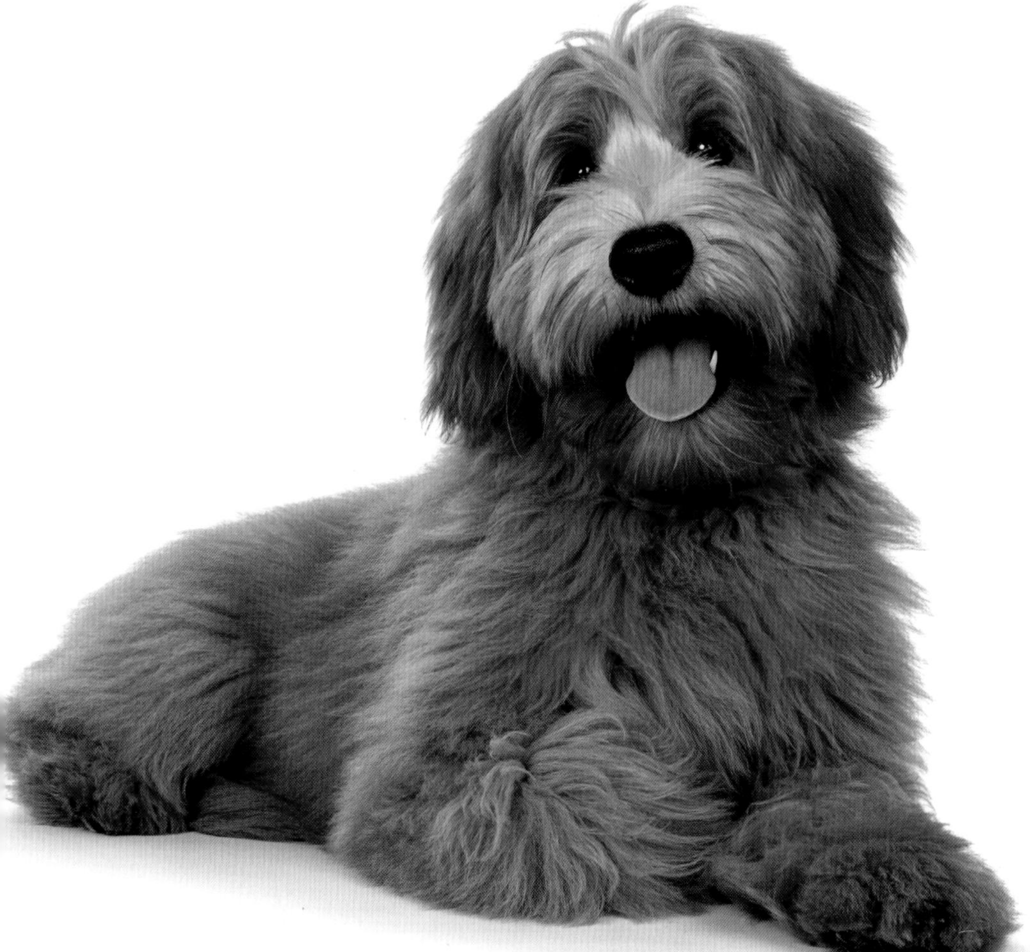

doll	duck
dress	dad
dig	dish
dog	